MUTUAL FUND INVESTORS

Common Mistakes & Myths

Vivek Kumar Bajaj

Mutual Fund Investor

3rd Edition

DISCLAIMER

"Mutual Fund investments are subject to market risk. Please read the offer document carefully before investing"

This book is only for educational purposes.

The author only shares his personal experiences and views. This book does not guarantee any profit. Take professional advice before implementing any idea mention here.

About the Author...

Vivek Kumar Bajaj is a Mutual fund distributor, insurance consultant and Income tax return advisor.

Vivek is working in the financial sector since 2002. He started his career as an insurance advisor with ICICI prudential life insurance. In these last 18 years, he works with a single motto, "Long term relationship with customers." Currently, he is working as a channel partner with prudent corporate advisory services.

He is passionate about spreading knowledge, which he accumulated in these 18 years. He works seven days a week for the betterment and profitability of his clients.

Beyond helping clients manage their investments, he likes spending time in nature and mountains. He loves safari and car drive in forest areas.

This book is dedicated to my better half, my brilliant and beautiful wife. She is the one without whom I am nothing. I am always thankful for her support, love and inspiration.

A Mutual Fund is a trust that collects money from investors who share a common financial goal and invest the proceeds in different asset classes, as defined by the investment objectives

----

INVESCO MF.COM

CONTENTS

FOREWORD

Investing is a mindset. If you tune your mind, you will find many good options near you. Mutual Funds are among one of them. You can beat inflation with Mutual Funds.

In the last ten years working as a Mutual Fund Distributor, many investors who want to invest in Mutual Funds choose to invest in some other products just because of a lack of knowledge. There is no one available to help them understand what Mutual Funds are and how it will fulfill their long-term goals.

Some investors start investing in Mutual Funds without proper knowledge and even don't know how Mutual Fund works.

This book is the first installment of my educational series focusing on three essential areas, i.e., understanding Mutual Funds in layman language, common mistakes which most investors do & myths relating to Mutual Funds.

If you are a retail Mutual Fund investor or plan to invest in Mutual Funds, this book will be of great help.

Happy Investing!

Vivek Kumar Bajaj

Author, IFA & Consultant

SECTION ONE - WHAT IS MUTUAL FUNDS

UNDERSTANDING MUTUAL FUNDS

WHAT ARE MUTUAL FUNDS?

Mutual Funds, as its name suggests, "A fund which is created mutually by a large number of investors, having common goals and objectives."

Let's Simplify

AMC create a fund to invest in Sensex's top 25 equity. Now fund invites investments via NFO (New Fund Offer) from investors having the same goals. All different investors put their money in a pool account and the fund invests that money in the top 25 listed shares as per the pre-designed portfolio.

While creating a fund, Mutual Funds must have clear objectives and investment strategy with a pre-designed portfolio. AMC will appoint a professional fund management team to manage investments.

ADVANTAGES OF MUTUAL FUNDS

Diversification

It means spreading your entire amount in different asset classes, i.e., some in equity, some in debt or gold and so on. While investing in one asset class, Mutual Funds diversify the investment in different scripts.

Let's Simplify

Mr. X wants to invest in equity. He has two options; either invest his money in any top 25 equity shares or invest in any equity Mutual Fund scheme (investing in top 25 equity shares). In the first option, the probability of the share price goes downwards is higher. If he chooses option two, the probability of all 25 shares goes downwards is lower.

By choosing option two, he can diversify his investments. If some shares go downwards, the others can compensate for the losses.

Regulated industry

SEBI, the stock market regulator, regulates the Mutual Funds. SEBI keeps an eye on all Mutual Funds to protect the interest of investors.

Minimal investments

Anyone can start investing in a very small amount of Rs.500 monthly. By investing a small amount in Mutual Funds, you can become a part of big scripts beyond the reach of small investors.

Qualified Professional management team

When you invest your money through Mutual Funds, a professionally qualified team will take care of your money. They have their research, analysis, observation, expertise and experiences. They will decide what to buy and when to buy.

Liquidity

In Mutual Funds, you always have the option to buy and sell Mutual Funds units except for close-ended and lock-in funds. Whenever you need money, you can withdraw your investment partially or fully. The fund will send your money within 3-10 days as per the fund norms.

Convenience

Once your KYC is submitted and registered, you can invest any time as per your convenience. You can use any online account available or your Demat account for investments.

If you want to invest manually, you can visit the registrar or AMC. You can start your investment with just Rs. 500/-.

Many options

You can choose your best-suited fund as per your requirement and investment needs. Different funds are available for the various asset classes, risk level and time horizon.

Transparency

In Mutual Funds, you will get full transparency regarding charges, brokerages and loads. You can quickly check how much amount is paid to different expenditure heads. Mutual Funds are also fully transparent regarding investments made in different stocks. Stocks available in the portfolio and their percentage holding are also available monthly.

DISADVANTAGES OF MUTUAL FUNDS

Exit loads

If you redeem or exit before the described period, i.e., exit load period, you need to pay the exit charges. Exit load varies from zero to 2% or higher in some funds. It's a penalty charged by Mutual Funds for leaving before the compilation of the exit load period. So it's advisable to read the offer document carefully before investing.

Fee and charges

Mutual Funds charged some fee for his professional services given and the fee structure is as per SEBI norms. All expenditure, including office expenditure, salaries, commissions, etc., is under the SEBI's pre-defined limit.

Risks

The risk is always there with Mutual Funds. In some Mutual Funds, there is market risk and in some credit or interest risk. Please discuss the risk with your Financial Advisor before investing.

No control

Investors don't have any control over the choices of shares or scripts buying by the fund. The fund manager's decision is always final.

TYPES OF MUTUAL FUNDS

Mutual Funds are considered a vast segment. If we classify funds as per their structure, there are two types:

1. Open-ended funds
   and
2. Closed-ended funds

Open-ended funds are those funds that are open for investments and available for exit anytime on any business day.

Closed-ended funds are those funds that have a pre-defined maturity date or exit date and open for investments at the time of NFO only. Entry and exit in these funds are prohibited after NFO and before the exit date.

If we classify funds as per the assets class, there are broadly two types:

1. Equity funds
   and
2. Debt funds

Equity Funds

Equity funds are those funds that invest in the company's shares. Types of equity funds are:

1. Large-cap funds, midcap funds, small-cap funds, multi-cap funds and micro-cap funds
2. Equity Linked saving schemes (Tax saver funds)
3. Sector funds
4. FOF (Fund of Funds)
5. Index funds
6. International funds

Debt Funds

Debt funds are those funds that invest in interest base papers, gold, debentures, etc. Types of debt funds are:

1. Liquid funds
2. Ultra short term funds
3. Short term funds
4. Medium-term funds
5. Floating rate funds

6. Overnight funds
7. Dynamic bond funds
8. Corporate bond funds
9. Gilt funds
10. Capital protection funds
11. Fixed maturity plans

Some funds are a mixture of equity and debt funds. These funds are called Hybrid funds. Types of hybrid funds are:

1. Balanced funds
2. Assets allocation funds
3. Equity savings funds
4. Balanced advantage funds
5. Monthly income plan

Investment options in Mutual Funds

In Mutual Fund investments, three different options are available. In terms of returns, all three are the same, but the taxability applicable is different. These options are growth, dividend payouts and dividend reinvest.

STRUCTURE AND WORKING OF MUTUAL FUNDS

Structure of Mutual Funds

The first person or entity who dreams about setting up a Mutual Fund is the sponsor. The sponsor applies for the license to set up a Mutual Fund. SEBI gives permission, and the sponsor creates a company which is called AMC (Asset Management Company).

As soon as an AMC is formed, it comes under the regulation of SEBI. The sponsor is the first investor and owns a significant stake. AMC seeks approval from SEBI to create a fund and appoint a trustee.

A trustee is an entity that acts as a guardian for the assets of a fund. The trustee appoints a custodian for the safekeeping of the assets of a fund.

AMC appoints a registrar to whom all operational processing work will outsource. AMC appoints distributors to sell the fund to the investors. AMC appoints Fund Manager to manage the fund.

AMC starts receiving funds through NFO (New Fund Offer) in a pool account under the trustee and invests through the pool account.

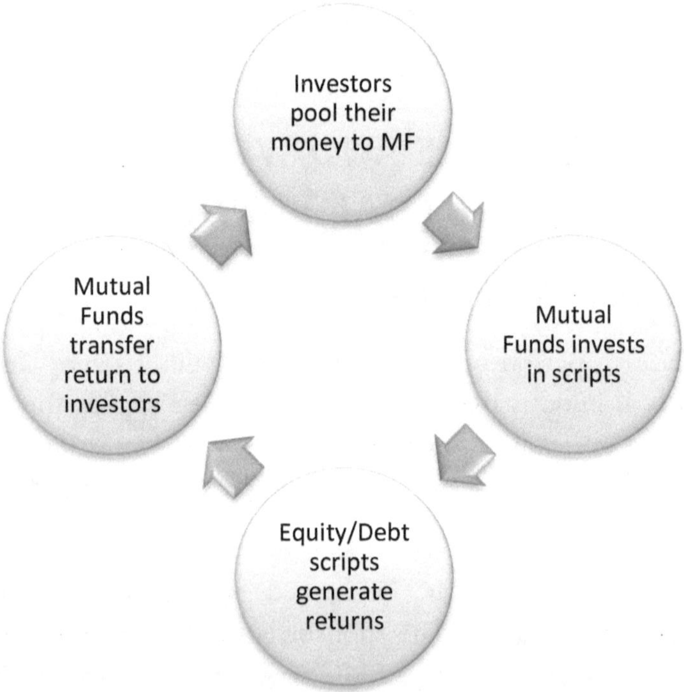

Figure 1: Working chart of Mutual Funds

HOPE YOU ARE ENJOYING READING MY BOOK. IF YOU LIKE TO RATE MY BOOK,

SCAN BELOW

UNDERSTANDING SYSTEMATIC PLANS AND NAV

SYSTEMATIC PLANS

SIP (SYSTEMATIC INVESTMENT PLAN)

SIP is the investment method in which the investor pre-orders his/her bank to pay a fixed amount to the Mutual Fund on a selected date every month.

There are two investment methods; one is a Lump sum (in this method, the investor invests the money which he earned already), and the second one is SIP.

In SIP, investors allocate some of his/her future earnings to Mutual Funds every month. Investor pre-defined the date and amount of investment and instructs his/her bank to pay regularly via auto debit or mandate till cancellation.

ADVANTAGES OF SIP

Discipline:

When you registered for a SIP, you only pre-order your bank to pay a fixed sum every month on a selected date. It will help to invest in a disciplined manner because the bank will not forget to pay the amount, and you will never miss investment.

Compounding:

You will get better returns in a longer period due to compounding. So it's always advisable to start investments as early as possible and always plan for the long term.

Convenience:

SIP allows you to start investments with a minimal monthly amount. You need not pay your monthly SIP amount by yourself every month. AMC will automatically deduct your monthly SIP amount from your bank account, so it's the most convenient way to invest in Mutual Funds.

Rupee Cost Averaging:

When you regularly invest through SIP, you will always in a buying position whether the market is up or down. Your buying price will be different every month so that you will get the best average cost per unit of your investments. A longer period will give the best average price for the entire period, and your gains will improve.

STP (SYSTEMATIC TRANSFER PLAN)

An STP investor instructs the Mutual Fund to regularly transfer a fixed amount on a specified date from one fund to another.

SWP (SYSTEMATIC WITHDRAWAL PLAN)

In SWP, the investor instructs Mutual Fund to withdraw a fixed amount on a specified date regularly and transfer the money to his/her bank account. It is also called the monthly withdrawal plan.

Let's Simplify

Suppose Mr. A wants to invest Rs. Five thousand monthly from his salary for the next ten years, he will choose SIP for the investment.

Suppose Mr. A wants to invest Rs. Five thousand monthly in XYZ fund from his prior investments in ABC fund, he will choose STP for the investment.

Suppose Mr. A wants to withdraw Rs. Five thousand monthly from his investments in ABC fund, he will choose SWP for the purpose.

UNDERSTANDING NAV

NAV is the Net Assets Value. The total market value of all the assets of a fund less liabilities on any business day divided by the number of units issued by the fund will become the NAV of that day.

Fund calculates NAV daily. NAV is just an indicator that gives an overview of the track of a fund. It is the price per unit of a fund on that business day.

Many investors have a myth that investments in lower NAV funds will increase the chances of profit. NAV has nothing to do with the profit or future performance of a fund.

Let's Simplify

Over time, if a fund's assets' market value increases, the NAV will show that growth. Growth is in a percentage. If the net asset increased by 10 percent, NAV also increased by 10 percent, whether NAV is 10 or 100. In the case of 10, NAV increased by one, and in the case of 100, NAV increased by 10.

LAW OF AVERAGING

How Law of Averaging impact equity Mutual Funds

First, we have to understand the Law of Average. When a particular article's rate is volatile, and the transaction happens many times in a specific time frame, you will get the average transaction price for that time range.

Let's Simplify

Mr. A invests Rs. 1000/- 12 times in a year. Each transaction's price was 10, 10.5, 11, 10.5, 9.5, 9, 8.5, 8, 8.5, 9, 9.5 and 10, respectively. The average price of this time range is 9.5, so Mr. A gets 1263.15 units in total.

Mr. A starts his investment at Rs.10 NAV and ends his investment at Rs. 10 NAV. The market price of his asset is Rs. 12631 against his investment of Rs. 12000. He got a profit of Rs. 631 while the NAV is at the starting level.

So the point is "Lower the Average price, Higher will be the Returns."

Let's take one more example.

Mr. X starts his SIP for 12 months for a value of Rs.10000/- pm. The NAV of a fund is Rs.100 at the time he started his investments. On the first SIP investment, he got 100 units. The NAV decreased thereafter and remaining 11 SIP invest at 95, 90, 92, 87, 89, 85, 80, 86, 88, 92 and 95 respectively. The average price of these transactions is Rs.89.916, and the total units received are 1334.57.

At the end of 12 months, the investment market value is Rs.126784.15 at the current price of Rs.95. Hence he has a profit of Rs.6784.15, whereas the NAV of a fund is down by Rs.5.

This method is called the power of averaging. So the point is, you as an investor must focus on the number of units and average price per unit. Better the average price, the higher will be the value of your fund.

The Law of Average is not only for the SIP, but lump-sum investors also use this tool to get a better price.

Let's Take One More Example.

Mr. Y invests Rs.10000/- Lump sum in a fund at the price of Rs.100 per unit. After his investment, the price of a fund goes down by Rs.10/-. So he decided to invest Rs.5000/- more in a fund at the cost of Rs.90/-. After some time, the price of a fund decreased again by Rs.15/-. So he again decided to invest Rs.10000/- in a fund at the cost of Rs.75/-.

After three years, the price of a fund is Rs.105/- and Mr. Y needs the money, so he decided to withdraw the fund. Now, if you calculate, the market value of the investment is Rs.30333/- against his investment of Rs.25000/-.

The fund's price is increased by just 5% in three years, but the value increased by more than 20% in these three years. This increase is because he gets extra units when the market is down.

The only point is that you have to focus on the number of units and average price per unit, and the returns will follow automatically.

UNDERSTANDING ASSET CLASS

An Asset Class is a grouping of investments that exhibit similar characteristics and are subject to the same laws and regulations. Equities (stocks), Fixed Income (bonds), cash and cash equivalents, real estate, commodities, futures, and other financial derivatives are examples of asset classes.

-Asset Class Definition by Investopedia

Let's Simplify

Defining asset class means categorizing funds as per the instruments where that fund invests. Mostly all instruments of the same asset class behave similarly and have common characteristics.

In Indian Mutual Funds, broadly, we have four types of asset class;

1. Equity
2. Fixed income instruments
3. Gold
4. Cash and money market instruments

Some Mutual Funds have real-estate funds also.

While creating a fund, Mutual Fund can have one or two major asset classes and one or two minor asset classes.

UNDERSTANDING RISK

Risk is the possibility or chance of loss, danger, or injury. An example of risk is a teenage boy on a car insurance policy.

-yourdicitionory.com

Let's Simplify

Risk is a chance of losing something, i.e., money, health, life, etc. Suppose you decide to do something and have a possibility of something wrong happening that wrong is a risk.

Risk in nature is uncertain, but you can reduce or minimize it with proper management.

WHAT IS RISK-TAKING CAPACITY?

If a person takes an informed decision knowing about the risk, this behavior is called risk-taking capacity. In simple words, if a person knows what he can lose, and he is ready to take a chance for the probability of gains, this is his risk-taking capacity.

KNOW YOURSELF

When we talk about Mutual Funds or investments, there is always a risk of losing money. Depending on an asset class, the risk may be lower or higher. For example, if we invest in bank FD, the risk of losing money is lower than investing in a company FD. So it's always advisable before taking any decision on investments *"Ask Yourself how much risk you can take."*

A higher return will always come with a higher risk. What is your risk-taking capacity? Never lie to yourself because one lie will damage your financial health. Freely ask yourself, are you ready to take a risk?

Risk is always there whether you go for traditional investments like bank fixed deposit, PPF, RD, Gold, etc., or you choose equity-based investments like Mutual Funds, Shares, private equity, etc. The volume of risk is different in all assets, some have lower risk, and some have a higher risk. The lower risk will give lower returns, and higher risk has the potential to generate higher returns. So don't lie to yourself and ask, *"how much risk."*

TYPES OF INVESTMENT RISK

When we talk about investments in Mutual Funds, there are nine types of risk associated;

1. **Market Risk:** It's a very common risk with Mutual Funds. If the market value of investments declines due to some government policies or other events that affect the entire market, it is market risk. There are three types of market risk; equity risk, interest rate risk and currency risk.

    a. **Equity risk:** This is a share price risk. The share market is highly volatile, and the prices of shares always go up and down depending on demand and supply. Equity risk is when your investments' market price goes down just because of the share price drop.

    b. **Interest rate risk:** This risk is associated with debt investments like debt Mutual Funds. This risk means a drop in the market value of assets due to a change in interest rates. If interest rates increases, the market value of investments decreases.

    c. **Currency risk:** This risk is associated with foreign investments or international Mutual Funds. If the market value of assets decreases due to the exchange rate change, this is called currency risk.

2. **Liquidity risk:** When you cannot liquidate your investments at a fair price and not get the money when you need it, this type of risk is liquidity risk. In Mutual Funds, investments in closed-ended funds, ELSS, FMP's are having this type of risk.

3. **Concentration risk:** This risk arises when you invest your money in one type of investment. Proper diversification will help you to manage this type of risk.

4. **Credit risk:** This type of risk is associated with debt funds. When a government entity or company cannot pay the interest and delay the principal at maturity due to financial crises, that are called credit risk. Credit rating helps to understand how much risk is associated with the investment.

5. **Reinvestment risk:** This risk comes in a picture when you want to reinvest your maturity value or interest income, or partial withdrawal. Due to a change in conditions, you would not get the returns equal to original investments.

6. **Inflation risk:** When your investments are not able to earn an income equal to inflation, and you are losing buying power due to low returns, this comes under inflation risk. Beating inflation is a big task, and only the good and managed investments can beat inflation.

7. **Horizon risk:** When your long term investment time horizon is altered due to some uncontrollable

events, it is called horizon risk. You can make proper provisions for the same and manage the risk.

8. **Longevity risk:** Living too long is also a risk because you need money to live and proper provisions for the expenses. You can eliminate this risk with proper retirement planning.

9. **Foreign investment risk:** While investing in international funds, this risk must be addressed. Losing investment in a foreign country due to a change in policies or relations between the countries will affect your investment returns.

RISK MANAGEMENT

The next question is if you ready to take the risk "*how to manage it.*" Risk management is a very crucial thing. There are many ways to manage, but regarding Mutual Funds, I suggest the following steps:

1. **Emergency fund:** First and most important thing is to create an emergency fund. This emergency fund will help you on rainy days. The value of the emergency fund must be at least six to nine months of your expenses. It will reduce your liquidity risk and horizon risk to a minimum. In the case of job loss or any other financial crisis, your monthly investments will continue, and household expenditure will also be taken care of.

2. **Opportunity fund:** By creating an opportunity fund, you can reduce market risk. In this fund, you must put at least 10 to 15 percent of your investments. This fund will help you to en-cash any opportunity in the market. Create this fund only when you are investing in equity or equity-related Mutual Funds. Whenever your investments have gains, book your profit and transfer it to the opportunity fund for future opportunities.

   Choose only low-risk investments with high liquidity, i.e., Bank FD, RD or liquid funds in Mutual Funds, while creating both funds.

   You can also use STP and SIP as a tool while investing in equity Mutual Funds. It will reduce your market risk.

3. **Diversification**: Diversification helps in managing credit risk, concentration risk and market risk. Try to diversify the investments in different segments, i.e., large-cap, midcap and small-cap. Also, invest in various sectors or choose diversified Mutual Funds. It will reduce the risk of loss.

UNDERSTANDING VOLATILITY

The market moves up and down due to demand and supply of shares or some other reason; this frequent movement is called volatility. Before starting an investment, some points that must keep in mind to understand volatility.

1. There are many reasons like global downfall or upswing, change in the central bank or government policies, any disaster, global economic disturbance, etc., causing market sentiments to move the market up or down.

2. Volatility means a series of ups and downs without any order or trend.

3. An investor can manage the volatility by keeping in mind these points. Invest without judging the

market, invest for a long term time horizon and have a disciplined investment approach.

Invest according to plan

If you want to cope-up with the market volatility, you must have a plan to invest for your long term financial needs and a strategy to execute that plan. Do not try to time the market; it will not increase your profits. Spend time in the market to understand the signals. The best strategy to handle the volatility, in my opinion, is, invest for a long-term time horizon and invest via SIP mode in a disciplined manner. Try to ignore market noises and stay calm in downfalls and upswings. Just focus on your financial goals and follow the strategy.

SECTION TWO - COMMON MISTAKES

SAVING IS NOT INVESTING

The most common mistake by many investors is that they count their savings as investments. First, you have to understand the difference between savings and investments. Savings is a part of your income, which is kept aside for some future expenditure. Savings will become investment when it starts earning some risk-free returns (Risk-free returns means, returns minus inflation). Now you have to understand that when your investments are not generating returns more than the inflation, you are losing money instead of earning.

Let's simplify

Mr. Z wants to buy a bike that costs Rs.60000 after two years on his 10th wedding anniversary. He fixed Rs.60000 at an annual interest rate of 7 percent.

After two years, the cost price of the bike increased by Rs.15000 due to inflation. Mr. Z received Rs. 68700 approx. as maturity value of his fixed deposit. So actually, Mr. Z loses Rs. 6300 as a buying power of his money due to inflation.

Therefore good investment is that investment that can generate risk-free returns.

Let's Understand With One More Example.

Mr. A and Mr. B both are working in a company and wish to buy a 10gram gold coin. The current price of a 10gram gold coin is Rs.36000.

Both started Rs.1000 monthly investment to buy a gold coin after 36 months. Mr. A starts his SIP in an equity mutual fund scheme, and Mr. B starts bank RD at 6 percent per annum for the same. Equity mutual funds can give more than 12 percent annualized returns.

After 36 months, the gold price increased, now 10grams gold coin costs Rs.43000.

Mr. B received Rs.39500 as maturity value. He loses the buying power of his money by Rs. 3500 in 36 months because his investment cannot beat the gold inflation in that 36 months.

Mr. A received Rs.43500 as maturity. His investments beat inflation, and now he has enough money to buy a gold coin at Rs.43000.

You must convert your savings into investments that can beat inflation and able to generate a risk-free return.

INVESTMENTS AS PER NON-PROFESSIONAL ADVICE

In India, people are very vocal about the products they used and those used by their friends. Advising is our hobby. We give free advice on any topic whether we understand that product or not; however, the matter is of someone's hard-earned money.

It is a matter of great worry that most of the investors invest their money on the advice of their loved ones, friends, colleagues and relatives. It is a big problem. Whenever you want to invest and need some advice, please go for professional advice. Non-professional advice will end-up your investments in a big mess.

As an investor, you need to understand that all products are not for everyone. If one product suits your brother, it's not necessary; it will work for you also. The advice is different for every individual, depending upon the risk-taking capacity and needs.

It's the matter of your hard-earned money; always ask for a unique portfolio from the professional advisor as per your need.

EMOTIONAL DECISIONS

As a human, we are very emotional. Emotions always play their part when we take any decision, so controlling your emotions is very difficult, but you can take the third party's help to prevent your wrong decision.

While investing, these emotions will always impact our decisions. We enter mostly at the wrong time and also quit at the wrong time.

Let's understand with an example.

Mr. A is a very knowledgeable investor. He invests according to his needs. He knows and understands the risk involved in investing.

When the share market's downfall starts, he started worrying but waits because he knows ups and downs are common in the share market.

After a regular decrease in the share market and his investments' market value, his emotions started overruling his knowledge. After some days, he decides to quit his investments.

This wrong decision gives him huge losses. After some days, the market recovered and started an upswing. Mr. A waits for the downfall to reinvest, but he again decides to invest in higher rates after some days.

His brains or knowledge does not make these decisions; the ruling factor is emotions. Thus these are emotional decisions. It's always advisable to stay invested in the downfall as downfall or upswing is part and parcel of the share market. The thumb rule is which goes down will come up, and which comes up will go down. Try to manage this volatility.

"In good times everyone invest, in adverse time does none. To the wise one who invests in bad times, wealth should come."

-Warren Buffett

One of the most common mistakes associated with emotions was investors invest when everyone earned, and the market is on the peak. After investing, if the market corrects or falls, they started worrying about investment and decide on quitting. The ordinary retail investor always invests at high and exit at low.

Always try to enter at low and exit at high. You need to stay calm when the market goes down.

FOCUSING ON SHORT TERM RETURNS

It is a human tendency that we always want the best for ourself. This behavior leads to a very common mistake by retail investors. While selecting funds they just go according to the short-term returns and rankings published in any website or newspaper.

You have to understand one thing, i.e., rankings and returns change very quickly. The fund in the top 10 today maybe drop down to the bottom 10 in a few weeks. The source publishing the ranking may have a biased opinion regarding top funds. You never know on what basis they ranked the funds and have a fair, unbiased view. Never select funds only just because of a ranking published somewhere. Always check long term returns and consistency. Rank the funds according to your needs and risk-taking capacity.

Chasing returns will not help you to create wealth in the long term. You have to stick to your investments at-least for some decent time. Your goal must be to accumulate units. A higher number of units will give higher returns.

CONSIDERING TECHNOLOGY AS KNOWLEDGE

Today the technology is very handy. Everything is in your pocket. But knowledge and experience are not handy. Many investors start behaving like fund managers after reading some articles. You need to understand the difference between technology and experience. You cannot swim after reading a book on "How to swim." Information given on different websites, articles and books are only for giving you an idea about investments.

SWITCHING INVESTMENTS REGULARLY

Investing in Mutual Funds is like planting a tree. You need to water it regularly and wait till the plant becomes a healthy tree. Now your tree is ready to give you fruits of your patience.

Most investors made this mistake; they switched investments from one fund to others to get higher returns and ended up with losses.

Switching is not a tool for returns; it's an option to adjust investments as per your risk-taking capacity. Never switch investments just because of some other fund showing higher returns. Always remember the thumb rule "buy and hold." Stick to your plan until and unless there is some issue regarding central bank policies or funds. If the atmosphere is not favorable to the fund, then you have to switch. Never switch your funds just because of market downfall or upswing.

GOAL-BASED PLANNING

Unplanned investments are just like no investments. In India, investment planning is mostly overlooked by schools and colleges. Therefore when people start earning, he/she is least bothered about proper investment planning. Due to a lack of knowledge, they make bad choices in taking loans, insurances and investing their hard-earned money. To understand goal-based planning and investing properly, you need to follow some simple steps before starting your investments.

Identify

Before starting your investments, you must identify your goals. Identifying means, you must set the goal or identify your need for investments. Bind that goal in the time horizon and estimated cost required at the time of fulfillment of your goal. Each person may have different goals or similar goals with different time horizons and costs.

> Let's Simplify With An Example.
>
> Mr. A wants to invest Rs. 10 lakh for his ten years daughter. His investment goal is the daughter's marriage, so he needs the money after 15 years, and the estimated cost of the wedding is Rs. 1 crore.

In this example, the identified goal is the daughter's marriage with a time horizon of 15 years and an estimated Rs. 1 crore cost.

Categorization of Goals

After identifying your goals, list them according to the time horizon in three categories.

1. **Short term goals:** All goals having a couple of years as time horizon are short term goals. For example, buying a car, getting married, planning a holiday, paying off any loan, etc.
2. **Medium-term goals:** All goals with a time horizon between 4 years and ten years are considered medium-term goals. For example, children, marriage and education, paying off housing loans, a family vacation at some special destination abroad, buying a bigger/second house, etc.
3. **Long-term goals:** All goals having a time horizon of more than ten years are long-term goals. For example, retirement, children's higher education/ marriage,

golden jubilee marriage anniversary vacation at some special destination, etc.

After setting up your goals, you can start your investments and choose plans as per your goal category. Some essential points must be addressed while setting up your goals.

Time horizon

While setting up your goals, the most crucial question to be asked is, "When you need the money?" The time horizon will impact the decisions and choices you have while selecting an investment vehicle. Different investment vehicles are available for different time horizons.

SMART goals

Your goals must be smart. While setting up and listing your goals, you must pay attention to some characteristics of the goal. Without these characteristics, the goal is not treated as financial goals.

1. **Specific:** Your goal must be exact. It must mention how much amount you need when you need it and from where you pay for that goal.
2. **Measurable:** Your goal must be measurable in terms of figures and amounts. Your goal must mention the amount you need to put in.
3. **Attainable:** Your goal must be achievable in terms of the time horizon and money you put in. It should not be too far from your reach. A slight stretch is an ok but not too much stretch as you quit trying.
4. **Realistic:** Your goal must be real. Imaginary or magical goals are not treated as financial goals.

5. **Time-Bound:** Your goals must be bound with the time horizon. It must have some specific timeline or deadline to be reached.

When you define your goals and earmarking your incomes to the goal, you must cut down some expenses and increase your investment amount. Just sit and ask yourself, "what are the unnecessary expenses which can be avoided or cut short." When we talk about investments commonly used formula is-

Income less expenditure = investments

But we have to think about a new formula.

Income less investments = expenditure

If you can work according to this new formula, you cut short your unnecessary expenditure and stretch your investments to accomplish your future goals.

TRYING TO TIME THE MARKET

It is a very common mistake made by investors. When the market is in downfall, they try to invest at the lowest point. But nobody knows the lowest point at that time. Theoretically, the highest return will generate if investments were made at the lowest point, but practically it's not possible. You cannot judge the current market is the lowest while standing right at that time. Only in the future you can understand the past market level is the lowest level.

Some investors wait to invest in the past lowest level to happen again in the future. But they never can invest.

So never missed the current opportunity and invest in downfall at current market levels because nobody knows the near future. As the market is a free flow, we never know which the lowest level is and the highest level. Investment with a plan or strategy is more important than market levels.

TOO MUCH FOCUS ON EQUITY FUND

As we all know, equity funds can generate significant returns. But we always forget "great returns come with great risk." As investors, we always want higher and quick returns, but we overlook the risk associated with it. Without understanding the risk-taking capacity, investors always focus on equity funds. If your goal is short term, you cannot risk the entire money. Always try to invest as per risk and time horizon. Sometimes average returns are better than risking the entire money in equity funds. Always invest as per requirements, not as per returns.

A mix of equity and debt funds can be a remarkable portfolio with good and consistent returns. In the upswing, the equity will generate returns, and in the downfall, debt will hold your portfolio valuations.

NEVER STOP SIP IN THE DOWNFALL

It is the common behavior of investors. They stop sip in downfall when the market rate is cheap, and you are getting some extra units. The downfall is just like a sale in a supermart. When units are available at the sale with some discounts, you stop buying. You need to understand that you will get extra units in downfall, and these extra units will help your portfolio generate returns. If you don't have these extra units, your portfolio will take extra time to generate returns.

Sip works on the averaging formula; the lower your average price, the higher your returns will be. At the time of downfall, every sip purchase lowers your average price and increases the chance of higher returns. If you stop buying at the time of downfall, the law of averaging will fail. So never stop sip in downfalls; even try to buy some extra units in running sip to lower your average price.

LOSING PATIENCE

Investing in Mutual Funds is like planting a tree. You start with seeds, put all your efforts and have patience till the plant becomes a tree. You have patience in all seasons, whether it's rain or dry summers. Whenever your plant needs extra care and attention, you provide it. One day your plant becomes a healthy tree, and you are ready to taste the fruits of your patience. The same patience is required when you invest in Mutual Funds for a goal.

Suppose you are investing for your daughter's marriage, and you choose a hybrid fund for the purpose. The time horizon is 18 years, and you start investing through the sip. In this case, the only strategy to achieve the goal is patience. If you continue your sip with patience for 18 years, you will achieve the goal and exit with good valuations despite all downfalls and upswings.

Most investors make this mistake; they lose their patience in downfalls or become greedy in upswings. In both the conditions, your goal is left unattended. Patience is the key factor for generating returns in downfalls and upswings.

OVER DIVERSIFICATION

Diversification is one of the most significant advantages of Mutual Funds, but it will become a mistake when an investor over diversify his/her portfolio. Over diversification means you invest in many funds of the same category with a small amount. It's challenging to monitor and track the investments in case of over-diversification.

Let's understand with an example.

Mr. A wants to invest Rs.10000 monthly in Mutual Funds. He invests in 20 funds of Rs. 500 monthly. Now, this type of portfolio is challenging to manage and track.

Let's Take One More Example.

Mr. X wants to invest Rs. 100000 in mutual funds. So he lists down 20 funds and invests Rs.5000 in each fund.

Over diversification is simply mismanagement of investments. If investments are not adequately managed or cannot track your investments, you always missed the opportunity to generate returns and end-up with losses.

NOT CREATING AN EMERGENCY FUND

An emergency fund is the backbone of your financial planning. Having an emergency fund ensures that you will never miss your sip due to any temporary financial instability. It will help you to achieve your financial goals.

As an investor, this is a very common mistake. Most investors don't plan for temporary financial crises. In the emergency fund, you must have provision for six to nine months of your expenditure. Put this money in a much-secured fund and never use it for any purpose other than emergency financial crises. In case of any financial crises, this fund will take care of your monthly expenditure, and you will never miss your sip.

Create an emergency fund before starting your investments. You can use any investment product where your capital is protected and have good liquidity.

COPYING OTHERS PORTFOLIO

It is a very common behavior of retail investors. They always want funds that their friends and relatives have. Some investors copy the entire portfolio of others. They still think my friend is earning more than me.

As an investor, you have to understand one point. Every individual has a different risk-taking capacity, goals and time horizon. Copying someone's portfolio will not help you until and unless you have the same goals, risk-taking ability and time horizon.

Copying a portfolio is like you start taking medicine for your injury, which is prescribed by a doctor for your friend's injury. Maybe the injury is the same, but both have different health and response to the medicine.

The same thing applies to investments. Your financial health and response to a particular market condition will be different from your friend.

If you are not able to control this behavior, you may suffer huge losses. If you need help with your portfolio, always ask for a professional Advisor.

NO APPLE TO APPLE COMPARISON

It is a very common behavior of new retail investors. Sometimes old investors with less knowledge and more technology also behave like this. They start talking about their investments with friends and relatives. How much you earn and in which fund these are the common questions. And conclude the discussion with the remark, "I have not earned in my fund, or my fund is not giving so much returns."

The point to understand, as an investor, is your fund is different from your friend's or relative's fund. Maybe the fund is the same, but the date of investment is different. If you want to compare your return with your friend's return, first adjust the difference between both investments.

Sometimes the comparison is between two different funds having different categories. If both funds belong to a different category, this comparison is null and void. It's like comparing the mango tree with a papaya tree. Both are having their advantages and disadvantages.

Always compare two funds in the same category, but remember both have a different portfolio and different strategies.

And never compare your investments with someone's portfolio. There is no such thing as "top funds with top returns." Always focus on consistency in returns. The list of top funds changed regularly.

SECTION THREE - MYTHS

LOW NAV IS GOOD

It is the top myth among investors. They always want to invest in funds having low nav. They believe that low NAV funds have higher chances of generating returns. The fact is NAV is nothing to do with returns. It's just an indicator that determines that at what point you enter and at what point you exit from a fund. It also helps to understand the valuation of the assets of a fund is growing or not.

Let's Understand With An Example.

Mr. A invests Rs.10000 in a fund having a NAV of Rs. 10, and Mr. B invests Rs.10000 in other funds having a NAV of Rs.100. Mr. A gets 1000 units, and Mr. B receives 100 units of that fund. Both funds have the same replica portfolio of Sensex. After one year, Sensex grows 15 percent. As both funds have a replica portfolio of Sensex, so both grow by 15 percent.

Now the NAV of the first fund grows from Rs. 10 to Rs.11.5, and the NAV of the second fund grows from Rs. 100 to Rs.115. Now see the valuation of both investments. Mr. A has 1000 units at Rs.11.5 per unit; the total current valuation is Rs. 11500. Mr. B has 100 units at Rs.115 per unit; his total current valuation is Rs.11500.

So whether the NAV is low or high, it has no impact on the returns of a fund.

MUTUAL FUNDS MEANS SHARE MARKET INVESTMENTS

It is a very common myth among conservative investors. As per their understanding, Mutual Funds only invest in equity. The fact is Mutual Funds are a basket of all types of asset classes. If you don't want to invest in equity, you can go for debt funds. Debt funds have low risk as compared to equity funds. There are different types of debt funds available in Mutual funds. As per your requirement, you can choose a fund from a variety of funds like liquid fund, short term fund, corporate bond fund, GILT fund, medium-term fund, gold fund, long term bond fund, etc.

In Mutual Fund, you can create your portfolio as per your choice and requirement. You can have different combinations of balanced and hybrid funds, starting from 10 percent equity. You can also consider multi-asset class funds, funds of funds (fund investing in other funds), international equity funds, etc.

MUTUAL FUNDS AND INVESTMENT PLANNING IS FOR RICH PERSONS

It is a very weird myth. Just because of our education system, we learn in schools and colleges how to earn only. No chapter teaches how to spend wisely and invest in your future. The fact is everyone needs planning, and Mutual Funds offer one of the lowest investment opportunities. In Mutual Funds, you can start your investment with only Rs.500 per month.

As far as investment planning is concerned, you need to learn how to plan your spending and avoid unnecessary debts. You need to understand how to convert your savings into investments for your future goals.

Mutual Funds are for everyone, small or big, wealthy or middle-class everyone will get something that suits your requirement. If you have dreams, start planning to achieve them, and Mutual Fund will help you to reach your desired goals.

DIVIDEND OPTION WILL GENERATE MORE RETURN THAN GROWTH OPTION

I cannot understand where these types of misconceptions come into an investor's mind. Mutual Fund offers two options, dividend and growth, for the convenience of the investor. These options have nothing to do with the return.

If an investor needs regular income, he/she can choose a dividend option. In this option, the fund will give some amount in a regular interval from the valuation. If the fund declares a 1 percent dividend, the NAV of the fund is reduced by 1 percent. The dividend doesn't mean profit from the fund; it's a part of your valuation, which is transferred to you.

If you choose the growth option, the fund will not declare any dividend. The valuation of your investments remains intact. If the fund generates any profit, that profit will also remain in your valuation.

Therefore the NAV of the growth option is higher than the dividend option.

Let's Understand With An Example.

Mr. A and Mr. B invest in the XYZ fund at the NAV of Rs. 10. Mr. A chooses a growth option, and Mr. B chooses the dividend option. In one year, the fund generates a return of 10 percent and declares a dividend of 5 percent on completing one year. Now let's see the NAV of both options.

Growth NAV at the end of one year is (Rs. 10 plus 10 percent) at Rs.11.

Dividend option NAV at the end of one year is (Rs.10 plus 10 percent less dividend paid) at Rs.10.5. Dividend paid 5 percent, which is Rs.0.5

BUYING TOP-RANKING FUNDS ENSURE BETTER RETURNS

It is again a very common and general myth among retail investors. They always want to invest in top-ranked funds. They move their investment from one fund to another as per the change in rankings. The fact is there is no such thing as "top-ranked funds." The ratings and ranking of funds change regularly. The fund in the top 10 this month can move to the bottom ten next month.

While investing and choosing a fund, you must consider your requirement and time horizon. You have to understand that rankings are as per the fund's past performance, and past performance cannot guarantee future performance. Always choose the fund which is more consistent in performance. If your account for ranking, go for long term ranking.

Always invest for the long term and stick to your decision. If you need help in choosing funds, take advice from a professional.

MUTUAL FUNDS ARE ONLY FOR LONG TERM

Mutual Fund is a very large segment. It has funds for every need, from overnight funds to long term horizon funds. It's just a myth that Mutual Funds are only for the long term.

Find below the list of commonly used funds for different time horizon;

1. The overnight fund is used for parking money for a couple of days.
2. Liquid fund is used for parking money for a couple of months.
3. Ultra short term fund is used for a very short term.
4. Short term fund is used for a couple of quarters.
5. The medium-term fund is also used for the investments having a time horizon from a couple of years to 5-6 years.

And if you have a long term goal, there are many funds to choose from.

Now you can clearly understand that you will get a plan for each and every time horizon in Mutual Fund. You just need to pick the right fund that suits your investments need.

YOU HAVE TO BUY MANY FUNDS

If you want to invest in a single fund, you can do that. Single fund investment will give you all benefits, i.e., diversification, averaging, compounding, etc. It's just a myth that you cannot generate returns if you invest in a single fund.

Your single fund investment will spread in different scripts as per the pre-designed portfolio of the fund. If you want to put some debt portion in your investment, you can choose one from different hybrid funds. If you want to invest in different market-caps, you can choose one from different multi-cap funds. And if you want to invest in a different asset class, you can choose one from different multi-asset funds.

Your single fund can fulfill your each and every need. You can reach or achieve your goals with ease by investing in a single fund.

COMMON TERMS

AMFI

The Association of Mutual Funds in India is an organization that sets standards and a code of conduct for the advisors. It takes care of all licensing, and every advisor is a member of the association.

SID

Scheme Information Document contains all the details of the scheme. It includes investment objective, asset allocation, risk factor and the investment strategy of the fund.

Addendums

If any details are mentioned in the SID change, the fund house issues the addendums. These appendices are published in national newspapers and also available on the fund house websites.

AMC

The Asset Management Company is responsible for the management of the assets of a fund. The AMC appoints the fund management team for the fund who take decisions relating to investments of a fund as per the details in SID.

Folio Number

Folio number is like a customer identification number to identify your investments with the respective Mutual Fund. Every Mutual Fund issues a different folio number.

SOA

Statement of Account is the complete statement showing all the information relating to the investor and his/her investments.

KYC

Know Your Customer is the identification process by the Mutual Fund. It's a one-time process. Once your KYC gets resister on KRA, you don't need to provide any document at the investment time.

KRA

KYC Registration Agency is the agency maintaining all information and records of the investors centrally.

R&T

Registrar and Transfer Agents are the trusts and institutions that take care of all the transactions of the investor. They keep records of all financial and non-financial transactions on behalf of Mutual Funds.

CAGR

Compounded Annualized Growth Rate is a formula to calculate the annual growth of a fund. As the returns of an equity fund are highly volatile, it's nearly impossible to compare two funds' returns. This formula helps to set the returns annually for all the funds for the ease of investors.

Absolute Returns

It's simply a normal return calculated on the investment without considering the time frame of investment. It shows a total increase or decrease in investment.

Exit Load

It's a fee charged by AMC. When you exit from a fund before the completion of the exit load period, the fund charged some penalty that is called exit load.

Expense Ratio

It's a percentage of the fund asset levied by Mutual Fund for the fund's expenses. It's an annual charge calculated and deducted daily. Regulator caps the expense ratio as per the fund size.

FMC

Fund Management Charge is the fee paid for the management of the fund as per the regulator norms.

THE CLOSURE

It's all starts with a dream. The dream to have lots of money to fulfill your wishes. In our education, nobody teaches us how to convert your dreams to goals. Once you learn how to set your goals, you start trying and focusing on how to achieve them.

Dreams and wishes are not goals until they are written as specific end results on paper

-Meir Liraz

Mutual Funds help you to achieve your financial goals. You just need to learn the magic of accumulation. If you follow some basic rules and strategies and avoid making some mistakes, you definitely achieve your goals and live your dreams.

In the long run, it's not just how much money you make that will determine your future prosperity. It's how much of that money you put to work by saving it and investing it.

-Peter Lynch

FREQUENTLY ASKED QUESTIONS (F.A.Q)

Q. When should I start investing in Mutual Funds?

There is a beautiful Chinese proverb, "The best time to plant a tree was 20 years ago. The second best time is now." So start investing today, it's never too late for a start.

Q. Do Mutual Funds invest only in stocks?

Are children's toy trains or roller coasters the first things that come to mind when you think of an amusement park? Most likely the former option. The fact that these rides are typically the most popular attractions in these parks contributes to a particular conception of what amusement parks are.

A similar misconception exists regarding "mutual funds," which is that they are risky investments because they only buy stocks. While this may be true of certain funds, many other types of mutual funds are available, such as bond funds and balanced funds that diversify your portfolio by buying a mix of stocks, bonds, and cash. Investing in mutual funds is not necessarily a risky endeavour; it simply requires an investor to do their research and understand which type of fund is the best fit for their investment goals.

Q. What are the indicators of risk in a Mutual Fund Scheme?

Before deciding on the best mutual fund scheme to invest your hard-earned money in, you must conduct thorough research. While investors frequently look at scheme categories and the top-performing schemes within those categories, they often overlook risk indicators for these schemes. When comparing schemes to choose from, don't miss out on their riskiness. It is important to understand that investments involve risks, and the success of any mutual fund depends on the risk management capabilities of its fund manager. Therefore, analyzing the portfolio of the scheme and understanding its asset allocation, style of investing, and risk management strategies is important to picking the right scheme. One must consider the level of risk taken by a scheme and not just its performance.

Q. Does one need an account in a Bank to invest in a Mutual Fund?

If you are wondering how to invest in a Mutual Fund, remember that it is mandatory to have an account with any bank and KYC/CKYC, PAN and Aadhaar cards. This has been made mandatory to ensure Mutual Funds are not used for money laundering purposes by a few unscrupulous investors. Furthermore, the government has introduced strict regulations to ensure that Mutual Funds are used as an investment avenue and not as a mode of black money conversion. Additionally, investing in a Mutual Fund is relatively simple and easy, as it involves no paperwork or hassles related to documentation.

Q. How do Mutual Funds help manage risk?

Risks take many different forms. A price risk, market risk, or company-specific risk exists, for instance, if you own stock in a company. Any of the aforementioned factors, or even a combination of these factors, could cause the share price of just that company to decline or even crash. In Mutual funds, the fund management team will work to reduce and manage all these risks. Diversification of stocks and bonds is one of many options. Mutual funds also allow investors to minimise risk by spreading their money among many different stocks and bonds.

Q. What are the Scheme Related Documents? What information do these documents provide?

There is a warning in every mutual fund advertisement to "Read all scheme-related documents carefully." What exactly are these papers? Key Information Memorandum (KIM), Scheme Information Document (SID), and Statement of Additional Information (SAI) are three crucial documents.

Q. Are Mutual Funds offered by Banks?

Savings and loans fall under the purview of banks, whereas investment is the primary function of mutual funds. When you invest your money in mutual funds as opposed to a savings account or a fixed deposit, you are making investments rather than savings. Savings can be accomplished by putting money in a savings account or a fixed deposit. Banking and mutual fund management are two entirely distinct industries, each of which calls for specialised knowledge of its respective domain and organisational structure. However, due to the growing popularity of mutual funds and the fact that banks do not wish to lose their customers, the banks have begun working as distribution agencies for mutual funds and providing their customers with a variety of different mutual fund schemes.

Q. What happens when the market falls midway while you have invested for a longer term?

Investors in mutual funds who make long-term investments through SIPs are frequently concerned about market declines during this time. SIPs are effectively built to reduce some mutual fund risks, such as volatility and market timing. By investing in a SIP at regular intervals, investors are able to average out the costs of their investments, reducing the risk of losses due to volatile market fluctuations. The concept of SIPs essentially allows an investor to purchase more mutual fund units when the market prices are low and fewer units when the market prices are high. This averaging effect of SIPs significantly reduces the volatility risk for mutual fund investors, allowing them to create a well-diversified portfolio that can grow over time and help generate returns on their investments.

Q. What is the correlation between risk and return?

"More risk, more return," as the saying goes in mutual funds. Is there truth in this? If 'risk' is measured as either, the probability of loss of capital or as swings and fluctuations in investment value, then asset classes like equity are undoubtedly the riskiest, and money in a savings bank account or in a government bond is of course least risky. By the same token, asset classes like equity also provide the greatest potential for returns, far greater than those provided by a savings bank account or a government bond. Hence, there is indeed some truth to the saying that more risk equals more return. But it's better to say, "More Calculated Risk means More Chances of High Returns".

Q. What happens when a Mutual Fund company shuts down / gets sold off?

Existing investors should take note of the serious implications that result when a mutual fund company is either put out of business or sold off. However, because SEBI oversees the management of mutual funds, events of this nature must adhere to a specific protocol. When a mutual fund company is sold off, existing investors need to be aware that their investments may be transferred to another company. The same is true if a mutual fund company is put out of business. In this case, SEBI has specific procedures that must be followed to ensure existing investors are not adversely affected.

Q. Why does the disclaimer say Mutual Funds are subject to market risk?

Mutual Funds invest in securities, and the type of securities they invest in is determined by the scheme's goal. An equity or growth fund, for instance, might invest in Company Stock. A liquid fund would put money into Commercial Paper and Certificates of Deposit. Similarly, a debt fund would invest in Government Securities, while a money market fund would invest in Treasury Bills. Each type of mutual fund scheme aims to deliver a return commensurate with the risks associated with it. Each mutual fund scheme has its own objectives, associated risks, and expected returns. And before investing in any mutual fund scheme, an investor must be aware of those risks.

Q. What happens when you miss SIP payments in between?

Many investors are concerned about losing money if they are unable to continue making SIP payments throughout their tenure. Such circumstances may occur for a variety of reasons, such as when you are experiencing financial difficulties or when you are uncertain about your job or business income. There are many options if you want to reinvest your missed sip amount; yes, you can do that. If you wish to leave or discontinue your running SIP, you may do so without penalty or charge. It's your money, and you can do whatever you want with it.

Q. Are Debt Funds risk-free?

It is a myth that debt funds are risk-free simply because they avoid investing in stocks. Debt funds are less risky than equity funds, but that doesn't mean they'll never lose money. In fact, debt funds are subject to market risk, which means their values can go up and down due to changes in interest rates. Thus, it is important to remember that even though debt funds are often considered to be less risky than equity funds, they can still cause losses if market conditions change.

Q. Do I need to understand stock, bond or money markets before I invest?

Imagine you have no other option but to take a plane to travel to a far-off country. What situations require knowledge of the various controls in order to operate the aircraft? or the different signals the pilot gets from the various control towers? Or how to use the radio equipment? Similarly to a mutual fund, you must understand the scheme in which you are investing rather than the entire mutual fund scenario. However, having a basic understanding of mutual funds will help you understand the scheme and its components.

Q. What happens to Mutual Fund Investments after the investor passes away?

Unless you have invested in a close-ended ELSS or other close-ended schemes like FMPs, mutual fund schemes typically don't have a maturity date. There is a term for which investments must be made on a regular basis, even in the case of a SIP.

In the case of an investor's death, all investments transfer to the nominee or legal heir. In such cases, the investment will remain in the mutual fund scheme until it is liquidated by the nominee or legal heir.

Q. How to choose a fund basis your risk appetite

Mutual Funds are market-linked investments that come with a variety of risks and unguaranteed returns. In addition to considering the investment objective and potential returns, choosing the best mutual fund also requires a risk assessment. Since each investor has a distinct personality, including a preference for risk, their choice of mutual funds will also be distinctive.

If you are not an expert or do not have sufficient knowledge, contact a mutual fund advisor for help.

Q. Are all Mutual Funds risky?

Every investment we make entails some level of risk, but the risk's nature and severity vary. The same holds true for mutual funds. When it comes to returns on investment, not all Mutual Fund schemes are equally risky. Depending on the investment objective, some Mutual Funds may be more aggressive than others, while other investments will be more conservative. However, regardless of how aggressive or conservative an investment may be, all Mutual Funds involve some level of risk. Consequently, investors need to consider their risk appetite before choosing the type of Mutual Fund scheme to invest in.

Q. Are fund managers necessary?

The answer is a big, unequivocal YES! It is crucial to keep in mind that generating strong performance relies heavily on experience in managing money and making investments. The likelihood of making profitable investment decisions increases with experience. Over time, this experience can result in a greater understanding of the markets and financial products, as well as help one develop the knowledge and skills necessary for success. Furthermore, having a better understanding of the markets and financial products can lead to more successful investments as well. The fund manager is the person with the expertise, knowledge, and experience required to make good investment decisions.

Q. What is KYC Process?

The term "Know Your Customer" (abbreviated as "KYC") refers to the Customer Identification Process that is a necessary step in opening an account with any financial institution. By using pertinent supporting documents, such as a required photo ID (such as a PAN card or an Aadhar card), address verification, and in-person verification (IPV), KYC establishes an investor's identity and address.

Q. How much of my investment can I withdraw?

Most mutual fund plans are open-end plans, which let investors withdraw their entire investment amount at any time without facing any time constraints. Only very rarely do schemes impose a restriction on redemption, as determined by the Board of Trustees, and only in exceptional cases.

Q. How often can I remove my money?

The ability of an investor to withdraw money from an open-ended scheme is unrestricted. All open-end schemes offer liquidity as a significant advantage, despite the fact that there occasionally may be an exit load that affects the total amount realised.

Q. Does long-term mean less risk?

Mutual fund investments require the right time horizon. The right time horizon not only increases the likelihood of receiving anticipated investment returns but also reduces investment risk. This is because the longer time horizon allows for the average rate of return to even out any potential negative returns. This is especially true for investors who have long-term goals, such as retirement or educational savings. Having the correct time horizon for mutual fund investments can have a major impact on their success.

Q. What are loads?

On a long-distance drive, a toll is occasionally collected as you approach the road or a bridge and occasionally as you leave. In order to recoup the costs of construction, the toll bridge company is frequently only permitted to charge the toll for a limited period of time. The business is not permitted to impose any additional tolls on the passengers after that time has passed. Same theory applies in mutual funds. A mutual fund scheme imposes a load to encourage investors to put money up for a period of time. After a certain amount of time, the load is no longer applicable. The mutual fund load is designed to reward long-term investors and incentivize them to stay invested for longer periods.

Q. What is Mutual Fund Dividend?

A mutual fund or stock may distribute its earnings as a dividend. Dividends are paid out under mutual fund schemes after the fund has realised a profit from the sale of securities included in its holdings.

Q. Can I remove money on all days or only on particular days?

Redeeming an open-end fund is possible every business day. A redemption request is processed the following business day if it is submitted to an Investor Service Centre on a day that is not a business day or after a set deadline, such as 3:00 p.m.

Q. Can Mutual Funds help create wealth?

Investing our money with people who are already wealthy or on their way to becoming wealthy enables us to amass wealth through the use of business and commerce. By purchasing the stock of various businesses, we have the opportunity to participate as investors in the ventures of other business owners. Shareholders benefit when business owners and managers are able to run their businesses in a way that is effective and makes money. This has the potential to create a mutually beneficial relationship between investors and business owners, since both can benefit financially from successful businesses.

Q. Aren't safe investments enough to meet financial goals?

One must keep in mind that the cost of various financial goals, in addition to the cost of regular expenses, will increase over the course of time. If the rate of inflation remains constant at 6% per year, the price of a goal will increase by approximately 200% after a period of approximately 12 years. On the other hand, if inflation is running at 7%, the doubling will take place in approximately ten years. With this in mind, it is important to consider how much more money may be needed in the future to achieve the same financial goals. Your safe investments hardly beat inflation, so how your are going to meet your goals. To meet these financial goals, it is important to consider more aggressive investments that will beat inflation and allow you to reach your desired outcome.

Q. Can minors invest in Mutual Funds?

Anyone who is younger than 18 years old is considered a minor and is only allowed to invest in mutual funds with the permission of their parents or legal guardians until they reach the age of 18. The minor must be the only account holder, and the parent or guardian must represent them as such.

Do Mutual Funds issue a passbook?

While banks and certain small savings schemes provide a passbook, mutual funds provide an account statement instead. The main purpose of a passbook is to keep track of all transactions with a bank: deposits, withdrawals, credit of interest etc. On the other hand, an account statement from a mutual fund includes details of all investments made, dividends earned, and withdrawals. As a result, a passbook is typically used to manage one's day-to-day financial operations, whereas an account statement from a mutual fund shows one's entire portfolio at any given time.

Q. Is it possible to change SIP amount every month?

No, in SIP you cannot change your monthly investments. But you can increase your investments by starting a new SIP or replacing the old one with a new one. With Systematic Investment Plans (SIP), you are locked in and instruct your bank to pay a fixed amount on a fixed date.

Q. What is Absolute Return?

Have you ever overheard anyone discussing their real estate investments? "In 2004, I spent 30 lakhs on that house.

Today, it is worth 1.2 crore! In 15 years, it has increased four times." An illustration of an absolute return is this. Absolute return is determined by comparing the final value of an investment to the price at which it was purchased. Growth over time is calculated in this way.

What is CAGR or Annualised Return?

A popular return metric is compound annual growth rate (CAGR), which accurately measures the return an investment earns year over year as opposed to absolute return, which measures the return an investment earns point to point without taking into account the time it took to earn that return.

Q. How to find the track record of a Mutual Fund?

The days of making significant life decisions without much knowledge—like buying a car or getting married—are long gone. Today, however, we have instant access to information. Mutual Funds are no different from other small decisions, such as what to order for the next meal, in that they are made only after extensive research or comparison. There are many websites that give you the track record of mutual funds. You can also visit the AMC website to download the required details.

Q. What is CAS? (Consolidated Account Statement)

A Consolidated Account Statement (CAS) is a physical statement that records all financial transactions made by an investor across various mutual funds during a month, much like a school report card that displays a student's performance on various exams taken throughout the academic year across various subjects taught by various teachers.

Why nomination is important in Mutual Funds and what is the process for it?

All of us have read historical accounts of kings and their fervent search for a suitable heir. It is advisable to designate an heir for each of your assets through the use of a legally enforceable will, much like how kings passed on their kingdom to the legitimate heir. Most people don't write a will while they are still living. You can write a will by following my step-by-step guide. By simply completing the nomination form, you can also nominate members of your family. Get your form from the appropriate AMC website.

*FAQ SOURCE: - www.mutualfundsahihai.com

HOPE YOU ENJOYED READING MY BOOK. IF YOU LIKE TO RATE MY BOOK,

SCAN BELOW

www.ingramcontent.com/pod-product-compliance
Lightning Source LLC
LaVergne TN
LVHW100332210926
848480LV00003B/1314